Thank you for your purchase of

LegeNDAry DRAGONS

Dragon coloring book for all ages

ISBN: 978-0-578-42009-7

Facebook: https://www.facebook.com/theecomicalartist

Follow me on Instagram@theecomicalartist

THIS BOOK BELONGS TO

_____

Use this space to practice your blending technique.

ABOUT THE AUTHOR

Kristy J Specht was born in Hastings, MN in 1983. She obtained her cosmetology license in 2009 and currently works as a hairstylist. In March 2017 she earned her Associates in Graphic Design and continues to do design work with coloring books and other design related projects. Her work is constantly evolving but she will continue illustrating books so others can share her passion for art.

OTHER BOOKS:

Colorful Critters
Untamed Ocean
Dinosaur Life

www.ingramcontent.com/pod-product-compliance
Lightning Source LLC
Chambersburg PA
CBHW081242020426
42331CB00013B/3271